For my friend and mentor,
Angela Blackwell, Ph.D., OTR, an expert on sensory needs,
who taught me to explore strengths-based strategies.

For my good pal,
Sophia Ansari, LPCC, RPT, who is always affirming,
holding space for me through continuous learning.

For my husband Bryce who encourages me to pursue
everything and anything my heart wants to do.

For the teachers and therapists who show up for kids like Mimi.
We are extra grateful for your love and advocacy.

I could go on and on, but the list would never end.
So, it's time to start the story and let the adventure begin!

Once upon a time, in a cozy little town,
There was a bunny named Mimi
who loved to hop around!

While she looked like other bunnies, she was different from the rest.

Mimi was neurodivergent and lived life with great zest!

Always full of energy,
  Mimi loved to explore.

She'd try anything once,
  never shying from more!

So when it was time
   to start school,
Mimi felt excited to go.

She couldn't wait to make new friends
     and share all the fun facts she knows!

But on the first day of school, it became very clear, that *this* little rabbit was *not* like her peers.

When Mimi got off the bus,
she began to spin, twirl, and hop!
But the bus driver yelled...

A cute little rabbit with a slight overbite,
Mimi loved to chew on almost anything in sight!

At recess,
other kids wore fancy shoes
and liked to run super-fast!
But Mimi liked the feel of her toes
being tickled by the grass.

While she knew the answers
to all of the questions,
blurting them out
caused trouble and tensions.

She found it hard to sit still
and squirmed in her seat.
Her mind would just wander;
it was hard to compete.

She left that first day feeling down with defeat.

Mimi wanted to like school and give it a try,
but she was always in trouble and didn't understand why.

"Do I have to go back?

I don't like it, you see.

There are too many rules!

It's so hard to be me."

Her mother gave her a loving squeeze,
reminding Mimi that she could do hard things.

When Mimi went into class,
she saw someone new...
A bushy-tailed teacher,
who didn't wear shoes!

With delight, Ms. McNutt,
soon came to find
that this little bunny had
a magnificent mind!

Not only smart,
but also quite speedy.
For her, solving problems
seemed to come easy.

When it came to learning, Ms. McNutt knew just what to do! She gave Mimi plenty of breaks and extra carrots to chew.

Mimi's focus grew better with a fidget in hand.

And she loved her new seat that let her wiggle or stand!

At story time, Ms. McNutt
gathered the whole class around,
and let Mimi play with her tail
as she read the book aloud.

MS. McNutt taught the kids it's okay to be different. It's okay to be you!

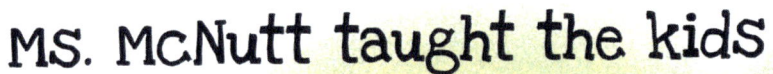

Some of us might love the feeling of touch.
While others may feel overwhelmed by too much!

But that doesn't make one way better or worse, it's our differences that make us unique and diverse!

When the book had been read,
everyone took their turn,
sharing their preferences
and what they had learned.

"I used to think that I wiggled TOO much, but now I know I learn best through movement and touch!"

The whole class discovered important lessons that day, to love themselves and accept their own special way.

Mimi was grateful to have a teacher who cared. Her confidence grew, and she felt much more prepared. Mimi became a star student, and her differences helped her advance...

"It's amazing what a little bunny can do when given a chance!"

Meet Mimi's Team:

Meet 'Quirky Kid' **Amy Nelson**, the creative force behind the heartwarming new children's book, Every Bunny Can Learn. As a Play Therapist™ and expert in neurodiversity and inclusion, Amy brings a fresh perspective to children's literature, celebrating strengths and promoting understanding. Her engaing storytelling and passion for helping children thrive make her a sought-after speaker at conferences and events nationwide.

Learn more at: emotionalmilestones.com

Yogesh Mahajan, a versatile artist from Mumbai, India, excels in various creative roles. As a storybook illustrator and animation film designer, he caters to both national and international clients, providing illustration services for print, animated TV shows, and mobile games. His exclusive crayon art style, tailored for kids' books, reflects his boundless passion and commitment, earning him a loyal and growing clientele.

Learn more at: animationwalayogi.in

Meet **Michael**, aka My Kewl Shorts. Michael is a talented songwriter and rapper who mastered his rhymes at 11 years old! Michael jumped on the chance to write a song for Mimi, believing, "It's cool to be different and use your natural talents to improve the world."

Download your FREE COPY of his rap at:
emotionalmilestones.com/Free2BMimi

Made in the USA
Middletown, DE
13 March 2024

51472954R00022